Less of Me

A 30-Day Devotional for
Your Weight Loss Journey

BECKY LEHMAN

Less of Me

Table of Contents

Introduction

Welcome to the newest phase of your weight loss journey! I know there are plenty of diets and weight loss programs out there, but this part of your journey may be set apart from the rest. I lost 100 pounds myself and, while I absolutely believe in the long list of benefits of eating well and moving regularly, I have also learned this goes far beyond those two things alone. Handing you a cookie cutter diet and exercise program might get you some temporary results but wouldn't get to the root of the problem.

You are fearfully and wonderfully made, a child of the one true King, and you were created for a purpose. Your unique body, flaws, imperfections and all, is a gift from your Heavenly Father to you, not to trap you or burden you, but to allow you to live freely in Him.

If you really want to lose weight and keep it off, let those Truths sink in. Instead of letting your decisions about your health be dictated by the number on the scale, let them be an act of love and gratitude to your Creator. My hope for you over the next 30 days is for you to experience more than just physical changes.

I pray as you read through these pages, you experience a heart transformation and fall more in love with God as you show yourself more grace and give your body more tender loving care.

Becky

Diet & Exercise

T he purpose of this devotional is to focus on a heart change, but some key elements are foundational for physical change in your weight loss that you want you to be aiming for every single day. As you go through these next 30 days, you want to incorporate as many of these things as you can, while at the same time extending grace toward yourself to cover the things you can't.

Depending on where you are in your weight loss journey, some of these things may be incredibly difficult for you, so do not try to flip your life upside-down overnight. The goal is a lasting lifestyle change, so every day, do the best you can, and let that be good enough. Over time, your best will keep getting better and better, so keep on moving forward, one step at a time!

I do need to emphasize that I am not a medical doctor, dietician, or nutritionist. I do not hold a degree in medicine, dietetics, or nutrition. I make no claims to any specialized medical training, nor do I dispense medical advice or prescriptions. This content is not intended to diagnose, cure, or treat any diseases. It is intended to provide informational, educational, and encouragement purposes only. Please consult with your wellness team, and then make your own well-informed decisions based upon what is best for you. You should seek the care of your doctor before starting a new exercise routine or before changing dietary or lifestyle habits. Only you and your doctor can determine what course of action is best for you and your particular needs.

1. Eat at least 5 servings of vegetables a day.
2. Drink at least 8 glasses of water a day.
3. Sleep at least 7 hours a night.
4. Get 150 minutes of moderate intensity cardio in every week, as well as two strength training sessions. Side note - this doesn't have to be as scary as it sounds! Brisk walking counts as cardio and just a few bodyweight exercises can check off that strength training session.
5. Find an accountability partner and talk regularly. Don't gloss over this one! It could be the one thing that really makes or breaks your progress here, so just reach out to someone. Ask this person to go through these next 30 days with you. Text, e-mail, or call every day and talk about what impacted you in that day's devotional.

LESS OF ME

*"Whoever finds their life will lose it, and whoever loses their life for
my sake will find it."*
- Matthew 10:39

I remember staring into the mirror, desperately wishing I had *less* weight to carry around, *less* belly rolls hanging over the side of my jeans, and *less* flap hanging underneath my outstretched arms. I spent years hiding in the back of pictures with only my head peeking out, attempting to cover my stomach with couch pillows at friends' houses, crossing my arms to hide my belly, and constantly trying to divert everyone's attention away from my weight. I thought that was all a weight loss journey was about - shedding those unwanted pieces of myself.

Sure, losing extra pounds is an important part, but as you slowly start to shed the pounds, something else comes in to take its place. You begin to slowly *gain* muscle, function, and strength. You add health, flexibility, stamina, and confidence, and as a result, you stop wishing yourself away and start living life more fully, more *joyfully*. It's less about losing yourself and more about adding quality to your life.

That's just how it works with Christ. We all have these ugly parts of our souls that we so desperately want to get rid of – guilt, shame, jealousy, bitterness, anger. Many of those pieces are probably tied to our weight and our body image. They are those inner places we have fiercely protected inside the depths of ourselves under lock and key. But when we invite God into our weight loss journey, we are trading our shame for freedom, unleashing power and light into those dark and hidden places.

Think about the life you want to gain more than the pieces of yourself you want to wish away. Make this journey about your relationship with God, admitting all of your struggles, pain, frustrations, and inadequacies, and draw nearer to Him.

There are both wonderful and difficult times that lie ahead on this journey you're embarking on, so I encourage you today to commit your plans to the Lord. Fix your eyes on Him. He's just waiting to give you all the strength you need to take these steps to take care of the Holy temple of your body that He has given to you.

Lord, thank You for this body You have given to me. I am choosing to take better care of myself starting right now, but I can't do this alone. You know how much I have struggled with my weight over the years because You have been by my side every step of the way. But today is different. Today, I am committing my weight loss journey to You. I've tried doing this my way, and it hasn't worked. I need more of You. Show me how I can best honor You with all of the choices I make affecting my body - from my eating to my sleep. I'm not doing this for a smaller dress size or a lower number on the scale any more. I am doing this to draw nearer to You. Amen.

Day 2

EQUIP YOURSELF WITH SCRIPTURE

"All Scripture is breathed out by God and profitable for teaching, for reproof, for correction, and for training in righteousness, that the man of God may be complete, equipped for every good work."
- 2 Timothy 3:16-17

God wants to see us succeed and break free from any weight struggles, food issues, insecurities, and anything else that may be holding us back from experiencing a full life of freedom in Him! He doesn't just expect us to instinctively know how to do this, though – He teaches us, empathizes with us, empowers us, and equips us through His Word.

It's how He encourages us, spurs us on, gives us direction, and shows us there is *always* hope, even when we can't see that it's there. Part of rewiring our mindset is filling our thoughts with Truth, and memorizing Scripture is the absolute best way to do that.

Whenever I go through a trying time or start a new venture, I find a verse which applies to the situation. I was quoting 1 Corinthians 9:24 as I crossed the finish line of my first half marathon, exhausted and limping. Proverbs 3:6 was the verse I leaned on during the devastating and uncertain days of my divorce. Galatians 5:22 is what calms me down whenever I start feeling impatient or frustrated.

Scripture gives you direction, hope, and power, while making sure you are aligning your sights with God's will. When things get tough and your world feels like it's closing in on you, those God-breathed words whisper peace and assurance. When stress and worry and doubt start to tear you down, those Truths ground you again and keep you moving forward.

Pick a verse that resonates with where you are right now and memorize it.

Lord, thank You for Your Word. You have given me a guidebook that has the answer to every single question in my life and in my health. Show me a verse in Your Word that I need right now and help me to commit it to memory. I want this to be the first thought that goes through my head in tough times. Amen.

ONE SMALL CHANGE

"And we know that in all things God works for the good of those who love him, who have been called according to his purpose."
- Romans 8:28

My highest weight was around 250 pounds. I very clearly remember the days when the thought of losing 100 pounds and flipping my entire lifestyle upside-down felt completely overwhelming and next to impossible. Most days, it felt like it wasn't even worth trying to achieve such a lofty goal. I was a couch potato and couldn't imagine willingly choosing to go on a walk. I loved massive slices of cake and biscuits & gravy, and I surely couldn't imagine a day where I would *willingly* choose vegetables over french fries.

But, one small change at a time, that day eventually came and that lofty goal became my new reality. Every small change you make is like shifting the rudder of a ship. If you move the rudder just one millimeter, you are going to change your end destination by hundreds of miles.

I know how tempting all of the loud weight loss advertisements are with their big promises and rapid results, but don't go for the drastic approach to flip your habits. You could go on a juicing cleanse (been there) or give up carbs (I've done that, too) and you will absolutely lose weight, but it takes slow and steady changes for your behavior to shift long-term.

Don't let the overwhelming nature of far-away goals or a fear of failure stop you in your tracks.

Losing weight takes time and persistence, and those small changes can feel so insignificant next to those big long-term goals. Each and every one of them matters. God is working in *all* things for your good - the good, the bad, the big, and right down to the smallest detail. It *all* matters, so take heart, and keep yourself moving forward, one decision at a time.

Lord, thank you for working every single detail of my life for my good. Help me to keep moving forward, one decision at a time, and recognizing my progress - even when it hasn't achieved my end goal. When I am feeling discouraged, keep reminding me You are still working – even when I don't see the results yet. Amen.

SIMPLY BEGIN

"If anyone, then, knows the good they ought to do and doesn't do it, it is sin for them."
- James 4:17

I am the master of *preparing* for action. I can spend weeks researching all of the details of the Whole 30, Weight Watchers, and the 30 Day Shred. I will make schedules, meal plans, and approved food lists, and order new gadgets, books, and equipment. But all of that is the easy part.

When it comes down to actually *moving forward* with all of the strategies I have so carefully laid out, I throw out, "I'll start tomorrow" or "I need to wait until this busy month is over." That's the thing about plans – they can trick you into feeling productive when you are really still just as stuck as you were when you started.

Don't wait until you have the newest exercise equipment, perfect eating plan, or a lull in your schedule (like that ever happens!)! Don't create grand plans that require you to keep procrastinating action. You know what you need to do, and *now* is the time to do it!

Instead of getting lost in intricate plans or a list of excuses, focus on *acting*. **Right now.** You don't need a magic formula to follow. I am quite sure you know of at least 5 things you could do today which you know would be good for you, so *go do them*! The question of *how* you start isn't nearly as important as simply beginning.

Lord, thank You for showing me the foods, exercises, and decisions that are good for me and honoring to You. I pray You will help me break through all of my planning and give me motivation to start living out those things right now. Spur me on to simply begin, no matter what that looks like or how unprepared I feel. I just need to take the first step. Amen.

Day 5

MOTIVATION MATTERS

"Whatever you do, work at it with all your heart, as working for the Lord, not for human masters, since you know that you will receive an inheritance from the Lord as a reward. It is the Lord Christ you are serving."
- Colossians 3:23-24

I originally started losing weight so I could get a boyfriend. I was convinced my excess weight was the missing link, and once I was skinny, the boys would all come running, and life would be perfect (*yikes*). Shockingly, that didn't keep me on a healthy path for long.

It was only when I dug deeper and started to realize honoring God with my body had a bigger impact on my weight loss than I had ever imagined. God cared about the food I ate, the amount I slept, and how much I moved my body. He was not judging my outward appearance, but I couldn't fully live out the life I was called to live without giving myself the right care and nourishment – it's how I was designed!

When our motivation is only skin deep, we can't expect it to keep us going when things get tough. There is no solid foundation for us to fall back on there! Sure, wanting to fit into that cute dress or lose 10 pounds before a best friend's wedding may spur us to action for a little while, but chances are it's not going to last.

You were given this amazing gift of a body that houses the Holy Spirit. It's with that body you speak words of encouragement, love on and serve people with your actions, and live out your life's calling. When you connect your choices for food, diet, and health with your relationship to God, it gives such a deeper purpose to every choice you make.

Lord, thank you for letting my weight loss journey be bigger than myself. It's about more than just pleasing others or being more attractive. I am investing my heart into this to work for You. Show me how my unhealthy choices have affected my relationship with You in the past and held me back from living out my calling.
Help me to move forward and draw near to You, in body, mind, and spirit. Amen.

Day 6

COMMUNITY

"And let us consider how we may spur one another on toward love and good deeds, not giving up meeting together, as some are in the habit of doing, but encouraging one another—and all the more as you see the Day approaching."
- Hebrews 10:24-25

Loneliness has been found to be twice as unhealthy as obesity. *Twice.* We were not designed to do life alone. God created us for community and meaningful relationships!

Most of us long for those deeper connections but struggle with actually making them. It's easy to say it's too inconvenient, you're too busy, you're an introvert so it's hard to meet people, or maybe you just struggle to let anyone in to because you don't want anyone else to see those places in your life where you are holding on to fear, shame, and embarrassment.

I am encouraging you right now to let someone in. Own your need for connection and do something to make it happen, and remember healthy relationships are never one-sided.

Be present. Do life alongside someone. Set aside your "to do" list and Netflix queue to ask a friend to go for a walk with you. Write someone a card to let them know you are thinking of them. Hug a friend, just because. Your support system can be an instrumental part of your weight loss if you let them in and ask for help. The people in your life who cheer you on, walk (or run!) alongside you, and make it easier for you to make the best choices for your health are amazing. Investing your time, energy, and emotions into another person is simultaneously the greatest love you can give and the greatest love you can receive.

If you haven't done so yet, find an accountability or prayer partner to come alongside you as you go through the rest of this devotional. It's easy to skim, gloss over things, procrastinate, and skip steps when you are doing things alone, but inviting someone else along on the journey adds a whole new level of depth, and you will get so much more out of it.

Lord, thank You for showing me glimpses of Your love through the intimate relationships in my life. Help me to nurture connections with people who glorify You. Give me the strength to be vulnerable, trust, and let people into the hidden places of my life. Help me to reach out to them when I need help and always have a heart for serving them, as well. Amen.

Day 7

DO YOU WANT TO GET WELL?

"When Jesus saw him lying there and learned that he had been in this condition for a long time, he asked him, 'Do you want to get well?'"
- John 5:6

I don't always handle change well. For the most part, I love things exactly the way they are, and I tend to hold on to them for as long as I can. That is all well and good, as long as what you are holding on to is something positive, but bad habits are just as easy, if not easier, to hang on to.

If we want life to be different, we can't keep living it exactly the same way we have been. We can't just stay within the confines of our comfort zones. We *have* to change our eating habits, our exercise, our routines, our environment, and maybe even our relationships to change our body and our life.

I talk to people all the time about self-sabotage in their weight loss journey. They start seeing that number on the scale dropping, and promptly undo what they had worked so hard to achieve. Change can be unnerving, even if it's for the better.

When you lose weight, things *will* change. You will have more energy, your body will change shape, your clothes will fit differently, and your habits will change. There are a thousand reasons why living a healthier life would benefit you, but those reasons do not matter one bit unless you want it badly enough.

There are exciting transformations for you ahead, but you won't be able to experience them if you keep clinging to old habits. Maybe it's your nightly pint of ice cream that you are holding on to, your secret candy stash, or even bitterness toward a family member.

Whatever physically or mentally unhealthy things you are hanging on to, let go of them today. Start fresh with new direction. *Want* to get well.

Lord, thank You for working miracles in my life. You have the power to transform my life and help me break free of the chains of my old, unhealthy habits. You never promised it would be an easy road free of temptations, but with You, I can overcome.
I lift my unhealthy habits up to You right now, even the ones I most want to hold on to, because, Father, I want to get well. Amen.

MORE VEGETABLES, MORE WATER

*"'Please test your servants for ten days: Give us nothing but vegetables
to eat and water to drink.'... At the end of the ten days they looked
healthier and better nourished than any of the young men who ate the
royal food."*
- Daniel 1:12 & 15

I f I ask 10 different people what healthy eating looks like for them,
chances are, I am going to get 10 different answers. "You absolutely
must go low carb to lose weight!" "Get rid of all the dairy in your
diet!" "This cayenne lemon water helped me lose 10 pounds!"

Fad diets and superfoods change constantly. There are some trends I can
get on board with (I think quinoa is one of the best foods ever) and others
I happily skip over (no butter in my coffee, please). There are, however,
two healthy habits that should be foundational to our diet. These are
trends that have survived centuries of being scientifically tested and
proven, and they are certainly not secret facts.

For a healthier diet, you should be eating more vegetables and drinking
more water.

That doesn't mean you have to be a vegetarian (I'm sure not!), but you
should probably be eating more vegetables than you are right now. When
you fill your plate, start with the vegetables. Your meats, whole grains, and

carbs should all be *sides*, while vegetables take up at least half of your dinner plate. You can still drink wine or soda, but those should be special treats, not your main source of hydration.

When you do those two things consistently, eat more vegetables and drink more water, you will feel a huge shift in your energy level. You will get sick less often and have fewer headaches. Your body will be able to function more efficiently, which puts you in a better mood, and makes it so much easier to live the life God is calling you to live!

Lord, thank You so much for creating nutritious foods that satisfy my hunger and help my body function at its best. Help me to reach for water and vegetables more often. When junk food and soda sound good, remind me of all of the benefits of making the healthier choice that will give my body what it needs most.

As I choose vegetables and water more and more, change my taste buds to crave those things more than any sugary treat. Amen.

Day 9

WHEN TEMPTATION COMES MY WAY

"No temptation has overtaken you except what is common to mankind. And God is faithful; he will not let you be tempted beyond what you can bear. But when you are tempted, he will also provide a way out so that you can endure it."
- 1 Corinthians 10:13

Most of the time, we know the choices we *should* be making. Have an apple instead of that candy bar for a snack. Go for a walk instead of plopping down on the couch. Go to bed for a full night of sleep instead of binge watching Netflix late at night.

But the right choice isn't always the one we *feel* like choosing, is it? It's easier to press snooze than to get out of bed and workout or to run through a drive thru instead of cooking dinner at home. And at night, when our willpower is all but gone and the ice cream is calling our name, it's hard to resist. That temptation has a way of sneaking in and convincing us that we are powerless. That resistance is futile and we are left with no other choice but to give in. *Have another cookie. And another. And just one more.*

Temptation pulls you away from God, and it's far bigger than just a cookie. It is an attraction to do something that you *know* is not good for you. When you train yourself to say no to temptations like an extra cookie, you are building your self-control to resist bigger and more harmful things trying to lure you away from God's will for your life. Once you train it, that willpower muscle will serve you well in every area of your life!

Do not forget you have His power on your side! He never promises us an easy life without struggle, but He does promise you - when you are tempted to make a choice that isn't good for your physical, mental, or spiritual well-being, there is *always* a way out. It may not be the most obvious choice or even the choice you feel like making at the time, but it's there. Just keep looking.

Lord, thank You for always giving me a way out when I am feeling tempted, whether in big or small ways. I don't have the power to resist it on my own, so I praise You for showing Your strength in my weakness. When temptation whispers, "you should give in.
It's just a little thing," strike those lies out of my mind and remind me of that bigger picture. Amen.

Day 10

ON FORBIDDEN FOODS

"'Do not handle! Do not taste! Do not touch!'? These rules, which have to do with things that are all destined to perish with use, are based on merely human commands and teachings. Such regulations indeed have an appearance of wisdom, and their self-imposed worship, their false humility and their harsh treatment of the body, but they lack any value in restraining sensual indulgence."
- Colossians 2:21-23

I love *everything* about Little Debbie's Nutty Bars. The taste, texture, and beautiful balance of peanut butter, wafer, and chocolate make them my perfect food and far from healthy. So, with every diet I have ever been on, my beloved Nutty Bars were the first things to go.

But forbidding food has never worked for me. When I ban my favorite food from my diet, I end up obsessing over it. I think about it. I dream about it. And I build it up so much in my mind that I end up believing just one more bite of that crispy goodness will be able to solve all of life's problems. And the diet usually ended with me eating an entire box in one sitting.

We never willfully worship those sweet treats, but when we create these arbitrary restrictions for ourselves, we give that dessert way too much power. It seems like the right thing to do. They are unhealthy, so the decision to cut that calorie-laden treat out of our diet appears to be a wise decision. A lack of sugary treats is certainly not what we would consider harsh treatment of the body, but making a food forbidden is extreme, and brings out our rebelliousness. That "no sweets" rule only makes us want it all that much more. It's not just a decision based on how it will affect our body. It's a mindset that affects every decision we make about food.

Instead of jumping from one extreme to another, focus on getting all of your fruits, vegetables, lean proteins, and whole grains in every day, and let yourself eat some treats along the way! You are much less likely to stuff yourself silly if that food isn't up there on a glorified pedestal.

Lord, thank You for creating delicious foods for me to savor and enjoy. Help me to step away from the rigid rules of dieting, so I can still appreciate those rich foods in moderation. Break any power that food has over me and help me to avoid overindulging, so I can fully appreciate those special treats. Amen.

Day 11

PORTION DISTORTION

∼⚬∼

"'I have the right to do anything,' you say--but not everything is beneficial. 'I have the right to do anything'--but I will not be mastered by anything."
- 1 Corinthians 6:12

God cares about what we eat. He cares about *all* of the tiniest details of our lives, but food has more influence on us than we give it credit for. Of course, we need to eat to survive, but the type and amount of food we eat can drastically impact our quality of life.

Food affects every single part of our bodies, including our brain. Therefore, food also affects our relationships, our energy levels, how we interact with others, our immune systems, our moods, and our emotional health. The food choices we make even affect our capacity to live as children of God. Sure, you're *allowed* to eat anything, but there are foods that just aren't as beneficial, and I'm sure you know which foods those are for you! They are the ones that master you – luring you in and convincing you that you need to eat them to be happy. They seem to be calling your name, convincing you to take just a few more bites and promising your stress, loneliness, and pain will all disappear. They are the ones that give you a stomachache and leave you sluggish and always wanting more. Those foods also just happen to be the ones that don't provide your body with the nutrients it needs. Food is not your master, so don't let it call the shots.

Even the richest foods do not taste as good after the first few bites, so slow yourself down. Don't ruin the foods you love by overeating them. Use a smaller plate, portion it out ahead of time, take time to actually taste what you are eating, and stop *before* you feel stuffed.

It's okay to eat treats every once in a while, but protect yourself from overindulging. It is time to take back the control those temptations have stolen away from you.

Lord, thank You for caring about every detail of my life, right down to the foods I put into my mouth. Help me to keep working on my self-control and reclaiming the choices that are mine, instead of letting my decisions be made by tempting foods. Teach me to pay attention to my body's signals and stop when I've had enough. Amen.

I DON'T HAVE TIME!

"But everything should be done in a fitting and orderly way."
- 1 Corinthians 14:40

It's easy to feel my schedule runs me more than I run my schedule. Commitments pile up in no time. Just one more shift at work because I could really use the money. Just one more volunteer opportunity a week because they really need someone to help out. Sure, I can bake a tray of cookies for that event. Yes, I can meet you for coffee in between dropping the kids off at soccer practice and going grocery shopping.

There are days that fly by because we were so busy that we barely had time to breathe. Yet, when evening comes and we look back on the day, we wonder how we could have done so much, yet still not actually gotten a single thing accomplished? Sometimes we don't even know where all of our time is going. Maybe it's spent endlessly scrolling through Pinterest or our Facebook newsfeeds. Maybe it was getting sucked into FarmVille or watching episode after episode of a new TV show. Maybe it was setting out to clean the kitchen, but within 5 minutes getting distracted and absorbed in a completely different task, forgetting all about the original plan. There will never be a lack of things pulling for your time, but even the worthiest causes and the most wonderful people will suck you dry if you let them. So, how are you supposed to survive in a world that always seems to be demanding one more thing?

Guard your time wisely. Know your priorities, and make sure your schedule reflects them. Learn how to say no when you need to. Spend time with God, focus on your family, connect with your closest friends, serve others, and make sure to schedule time for your own health. If your body and mind aren't being taken care of, all of those other tasks get exponentially more difficult. Today is such a precious gift. Don't forget to cherish it.

> **Lord**, thank You for the gift of time. When I say, "I don't have time," what I really mean is, "I've committed the time I've been given to things already." Help me to make sure that the way I'm spending my time always aligns with my top priorities, honoring You above all. If something doesn't fit in Your plan, give me the strength to say no. Help me reclaim the power over my planner, instead of letting my schedule call the shots and run me ragged. Amen.

MOVE YOURSELF

"Do you not know that your bodies are temples of the Holy Spirit, who is in you, whom you have received from God? You are not your own; you were bought at a price. Therefore honor God with your bodies."
-1 Corinthians 6:19-20

We were lovingly knit together by a creator, and these bodies of ours are a precious gift. We are blessed to be able to walk, run, dance, swim, jump, and twirl! One of the best ways we can treat our bodies well is by moving, and moving regularly in our everyday life. Our culture is all about telling us to exercise so we will be bikini-ready by summer, have sculpted abs, and attract the most attention from men. God doesn't measure our worth by looking at our clothing size, the number of ripples on our abs, and especially not the number of people who find us attractive. The goal of exercise should not be about attracting attention, but about taking care of the gift we've been given so that we can live fully for God. It's not about how we look, it's about what we do with that gift.

When you treat your body well out of gratitude to Him, it even becomes an act of worship! Strengthen your arms so that they can twirl your children and grandchildren. Walk, run, and play to live longer, feel better, and be sick less often. Exercise because it is the number one thing you can do for brain health, memory, mental health, and preventing Alzheimer's.

How you move doesn't matter, as long as you are moving regularly. It doesn't have to fit into a one-hour "gym" slot on your schedule. Weave exercise and movement into your regular life, and it won't feel nearly as intimidating or tedious.

Lord, thank You for giving me this body. I don't always appreciate it as a handcrafted gift, but I want to start treating my body better than I have. Show me ways to move more often, not just to lose weight, but to make sure I am doing the things I can to stay healthy, both inside and out. Teach me how to make exercise an act of worship that glorifies You. Amen.

$\mathcal{D}ay\ 14$

BE STRONG

❦

"She sets about her work vigorously; her arms are strong for her tasks."
- Proverbs 31:17

I am not a physically strong person. My arms have always been especially weak, and despite significant effort, I still cannot do push-ups with the beautifully perfect form of the ripped trainers on TV. For a long time, I let that stop me from doing any strength training at all because I felt like it was useless to keep doing the same thing over and over again without the results. I felt like a failure, and a weak one at that!

Just because I wasn't getting the result I wanted, didn't make the effort count any less. I just had my eyes set on the wrong goal, which killed my motivation to follow through. God doesn't care if I look like a body builder or can do a one-armed pushup with my eyes closed. He is not impressed by outward appearances. He cares about my heart and my quality of life.

Strength training is important, and I highly recommend doing it at least twice a week. It is not a quick fix, but it helps you lose the weight and keep it off. It prevents diseases and improves bone density, reduces blood pressure, and reduces lower back pain – all things that help as you age. It also just makes your normal activities that much easier, like lifting the bag of dog food or picking up kids.

Every time you do things to build your muscles, your body is significantly changing and transforming on a cellular level. Just because you can't see the changes, doesn't mean they're not happening! Even if it's just incorporating a few exercises in at a time, do *something* to build that strength.

Lord, thank You for creating such an intricately complex body that works for me around the clock. Show me how I can strengthen my muscles to do the tasks You've asked me to do in life, as well as to take care of all of the functions I can't even see going on inside my body at any given moment.
When I'm discouraged and tempted to stop, remind me of the real reason I'm doing it - I am working for You with all of my heart, soul, mind, and strength. Amen.

Day 15

TAKE CARE OF YOURSELF

෴

"Come to me, all you who are weary and burdened, and I will give you rest." - Matthew 11:28

You know the lesson flight attendants give right before your plane takes off? Fasten your seatbelt, tray tables up, and in case of an emergency, put your oxygen mask on first. Of course, the reason behind that is because if I can't breathe myself, then I am going to be pretty useless to help anyone else around me.

This is not a new concept, taking care of ourselves, so that we can better take care of others, but it is one often ignored and pushed to the bottom of our to-do lists. If someone else's needs come up, that's usually the first thing to go. Taking care of ourselves is not selfish, it's good stewardship. It's a ministry and a service to others.

There are always going to be excuses not to, but it is absolutely critical that taking care of you is high on your priority list. You won't be able to be the best wife you can be, the best mom you can be, the best coworker, or Christian you can be without investing time and energy into yourself.

Rest is not a luxury; it is a necessity! You simply cannot have the energy, the stamina, or the clarity you need without making sure your own physical, emotional, and spiritual needs are met. Don't just wait for extra time to fall into your lap before you make it happen. Make it a priority and schedule it into your day. True peace, rest, and contentment are found in God's presence. By quieting your frenzied thoughts with sweet truths of His Word, you can find stillness. Take a step of trust, knowing God has everything under control.

Lord, thank You for being my ultimate source of rest. Help me to recognize when I am overcommitting myself and ignoring my own needs. Instead of reaching for yet another cup of coffee to keep myself going, teach me to be able to stop and show me what it looks like to find my rest in You. Amen.

Day 16

PLEASE, FIND ME BEAUTIFUL

"Your beauty should not come from outward adornment, such as elaborate hairstyles and the wearing of gold jewelry or fine clothes. Rather, it should be that of your inner self, the unfading beauty of a gentle and quiet spirit, which is of great worth in God's sight."
- 1 Peter 3:3-4

It's one thing to hear, "True beauty comes from the inside," but it's entirely another to actually believe it. I heard, "You have pretty eyes" for years, which is really just code for, "I don't know what to compliment about the rest of you" (or at least that's how I interpreted it). It was devastating to me and I craved the words, "You are so beautiful" - not as a consolation to make me feel better, but because someone genuinely found me attractive.

The problem is that "beauty" is subjective, so we end up setting unrealistic standards for ourselves. What I find beautiful might not be attractive to you at all and vice versa. Beautiful women look completely different from one culture to another, so whose standards are you trying to measure up to?

Chances are, you've set some pretty lofty expectations for yourself. When you desire to look just like someone else, you end up taking your uniqueness for granted. By critiquing your body so harshly, you end up unintentionally slandering God's creation, practically telling Him that He must have made a mistake when He made you (by the way, He didn't).

I am not going to tell you to write, "I am beautiful" on your mirror, because that still sends the message your physical attributes define your worth. Instead, I want you to start redefining the word according to God. What makes you beautiful in His eyes, the kind of beautiful that will never wrinkle or sag?

Lord, thank You for creating me exactly the way I am. Help me to see myself through Your eyes, seeing the beauty and purpose behind every "flaw" that I dwell on. Show me what You find truly beautiful about me and speak it so loudly that it drowns out all of the other voices telling me I don't live up to this world's standard of beauty. Amen.

THE COMPARISON TRAP

"Am I now trying to win the approval of human beings, or of God? Or am I trying to please people? If I were still trying to please people, I would not be a servant of Christ."
- Galatians 1:10

She is so skinny. I wish my hair looked like that. It's like she can eat whatever she wants and never gain an ounce – so not fair! I wish I had her body, her family, her friends, her life.

It's far too easy to look around and pick out the best parts of everyone else that we wish we had for ourselves, thinking you could concoct a better version of yourself by taking traits from everybody else.

It's a dangerous game to play when we start comparing our life to others', especially if we're assuming their life is fully portrayed by their perfect happy Facebook photos! We don't know the whole story of their lives, and chances are, we probably wouldn't want to trade places with them if we fully understood their story.

Jealousy has a way of blinding us to all of the things that are there, but we don't want to see. It steals our gratitude right out from under us, because instead of counting the numerous blessings we already have in our own lives, all we can see is what we *don't* have. Comparison is a recipe for disaster, and it robs us of contentment and joy.

It's not a bad thing to strive to do better, but do it with the goal to honor Christ! Doing something so that you can be just like somebody else or win someone's approval is just silly. No matter how hard you try, you are not going to be somebody else, because you were made uniquely you!

Praise God you are not just another cookie cutter copy of everybody else! Each and every person has individual strengths and talents that set them apart from everybody else. You have a specific job as part of the body of Christ that nobody else can do. Wear that identity with a thankful heart! Work on genuinely appreciating what you have and who you are.

Lord, thank You for not making us all the same. Help me to use gratitude to fight back against any jealousy that might creep into my thoughts. I don't want to waste my life wishing for things I don't have. I want to have a heart overflowing with thankfulness for all of the things You have given me. Help me to uncover my unique talents and strengths, and not be distracted by longing for others' gifts along the way. Amen.

Day 18

WORTHY

༄

For you created my inmost being; you knit me together in my mother's
womb. I praise you because I am fearfully and wonderfully made;
your works are wonderful, I know that full well.
- Psalm 139:13-14

There was a time I remember looking at myself in the mirror and seeing only flaws. I scrutinized my appearance in every way – my thighs were too fat, my stomach was too lumpy, my hair was too frizzy and far too curly. Not one feature escaped my critique.

It's hard to praise God for a body that you dislike, and even resent, but a heart of thankfulness was what I desired. Even after losing 100 pounds, I could very easily find fault all over my body if I looked for it (and I wouldn't have to look very hard). It is a choice to look for imperfections, just as it is a choice to look for things to be grateful for. Now, I make it an intentional decision to look for the good, for God's gifts, even in my appearance.

I thank him for fingers that can communicate with sign language, legs that can run 5ks, arms that can swing my niece and nephew through the air, taste buds that savor chocolate, lips that can curl into a smile, vocal chords that can sing, and so much more.

We are so dearly loved by God, not because of anything we've done, but simply because of who we are. Even in the midst of our sin, we were worth dying for. The deepest and darkest sins of our lives have been forgiven and taken from us, as far as the east is from the west. Instead of being covered by shame, we are clothed with the righteousness of Jesus!

Choose to see your value. You are important. You are not a mistake. You are created with unique strengths and weaknesses, set apart to live for a purpose. Don't believe anything less. You, dear one, are fearfully and wonderfully made.

> **Lord**, thank You for knitting me together so wonderfully. I am so easily distracted by the labels people give me, or I give myself, that I forget to rest in the fact that You created me and You don't make mistakes. Help me to stop trying so hard to win admiration, affection, and attention, and just rest in the unfailing security blanket of your unending love for me. Amen.

Day 19

FIGHT BACK AGAINST STRESS

∽✑⌐

"Do not be anxious about anything, but in every situation, by prayer and petition, with thanksgiving, present your requests to God. And the peace of God, which transcends all understanding, will guard your hearts and your minds in Christ Jesus."
- Philippians 4:6-7

Did you know experts estimate our minds think between 60,000 and 80,000 thoughts a day? That is 80,000 opportunities for our thoughts to wander! If we let down our guard completely, does our mind tend to wander to the positive or the negative?

It's no wonder stress sweeps into our lives like a whirlwind and sweeps us into a dark and tangled forest of endless "what ifs" before we even know what hit us. If we just sit back and let stress take over, it inevitably will. Our thoughts easily spiral completely out of control as we imagine countless worst case scenarios, most of which will never happen!

Worrying can trick us into feeling like we are helping the situation in some way, when really we are just needlessly driving ourselves crazy in an attempt to single-handedly solve all of the problems of the world. It keeps us both overwhelmed and completely stuck. That's not the life God intends for us to have.

But there is hope! If you choose to seek Him and ask for His help, even in the midst of the most painful and intense situation, He promises to protect your heart and mind. But it takes intentionality. It doesn't just happen. Counter your thoughts and fears with God's Word.

When you say, I'm just too tired, God replies, "I will give you rest" (Matthew 11:28). When you think, I just can't do it anymore, God responds, "You can do all things with my strength" (Isaiah 40:29, 2 Thess. 3:3-5) And when we seek Him, He replaces our stress and anxiety with a peace that passes all of our understanding (Matthew 6:33-34). God is ready and willing to take your stress and anxiety upon Himself. He is patiently waiting to strengthen you with everything you need, but you have to be willing to take His hand.

Lord, thank You for Your peace that passes all understanding! When worry starts to sneak into my mind, help me to recognize it immediately. Instead of letting my mind wander to worst case scenarios or running to the Internet or self-help books to find answers, teach me to run straight to You in prayer. Amen.

Day 20

STEP AWAY FROM THE SCALE

"Therefore we do not lose heart. Though outwardly we are wasting away, yet inwardly we are being renewed day by day."
- 2 Corinthians 4:16

There was a time when I was stepping on the scale at least five times a day. If it showed a number I liked, I would rejoice, celebrate with a cookie, and be in a fabulous mood for the rest of the day. If it showed I had gained even one tenth of a pound, I would immediately start doing jumping jacks, eat celery for dinner, and get quite grumpy for the rest of the evening.

We do not need to give the scale that kind of power over our lives! It can be useful for showing us a starting point and giving us a general idea of where our health stands, but the scale is not a real time measurement of the choices we make. It's more like the representation of our usual choices, our habits and routines. There were days I ate nothing but chips and soda and spent all day laying on the couch, and the scale showed I had lost weight. Other days when I had eaten fruit, vegetables, and chicken breast, and spent two hours at the gym, it said I had gained.

There are a lot of reasons behind weight fluctuations, but don't get hung up on them. There is so much more going on inside of your body than can be expressed in a number. I recommend spacing out your weigh-ins (once a month is plenty for me) because long-term changes are the goal.

In that in-between time, instead of measuring your progress by the number on the scale, try asking yourself these questions: Did I make the best choices I could today? How am I feeling? What can I do better tomorrow?

God certainly doesn't measure your success in numbers! He is looking at your heart and your relationship with Him, not your pant size. He measures success by our obedience and faithfulness to Him, and whether we are accomplishing His purposes in our lives.

Lord, thank You for not defining my success by my weight and for renewing me daily. Help me to step away from obsessively weighing myself and start finding other ways to measure my progress.
Keep reminding me this journey is not about what is going on in my outward appearance but has everything to do with drawing nearer in relationship to You. Amen.

EMOTIONAL EATING

"And my God will meet all your needs according to the riches of his glory in Christ Jesus."
- Philippians 4:19

Overeaters anonymous has a phrase they use to help their members improve their emotional eating – HALT. It stands for four questions they want you to ask yourself before you actually eat. Are you Hungry? Angry? Lonely? Tired?

There is a long list of emotions that can send us running to the snack shelf, but I love their reminder just to pause before actually eating. In that moment, when we are craving food so fiercely, we stop thinking logically, and we unintentionally boost food up to the role of an idol in our life by deciding it is the one thing that will meet our deepest needs.

We are not going to find true companionship in a pint of ice cream, and we will not find real happiness at the bottom of a bag of chips. Sure, we may feel better for a few minutes, but it doesn't solve the real problem, and the consequences are just not worth it.

Start to retrain yourself. When you know it's something other than hunger driving you to snack, stop. The greatest solution of all is to seek God first. Tell Him you are struggling, you want to change this bad habit, and ask

Him for help. We talked about the importance of Scripture on Day 2, and when you are in the middle of a battle with emotional eating, you need the power of Truth (I highly suggest 1 Corinthians 10:13 for situations like these). No matter what void in your heart or your life you are trying to fill with food, God can fill it.

Before you take a bite, ask yourself what emotion you are feeling and why. Think of a few ways you could actually meet that need, instead of just opting for a Band-Aid solution. If you are feeling lonely, reach out and call a friend. If you are tired, take a nap.

When you become more self-aware and more mindful, you have more power to stop the behavior.

Lord, thank You for meeting all of my needs. You created me to love You above all things and anything else I try to use to fill those spaces of my life are just cheap substitutes that will never satisfy. Help me to break the chains of eating when I am overcome with emotion. Give me the power to say no to old habits and seek You first before any other solution. When I am tempted, show me the way out and I will follow You. Amen.

Day 22

MORE THAN CONQUERORS

❧

No, in all these things we are more than conquerors through him who loved us.
- Romans 8:37

The biggest problems in life have a way of whispering lies to us. *I am too big for you to handle. You've already struggled with me this long, what makes you think you'll be able to win this time? You've failed before, so you might as well just stop trying.*

It's hard enough to change all of those unhealthy habits in our lives – getting ourselves to exercise more, drink more water, and eat more vegetables. When our thoughts are constantly working against us, they can leave us feeling hopeless and defeated, robbing us of our confidence and joy.

You were *made for more.* All of those fears and doubts about yourself are holding you back from living a life of true freedom in Christ, and you have all of the power you need to break those chains!

Being more than a conqueror means you not only have the power to overcome the difficulties in your life, but you will be *overwhelmingly* victorious! God cares deeply about the things you struggle with, but none of them worry Him a bit. This is the God who created the heavens and the earth, and the Christ who defeated the grave! In *all* things, you can have the confidence you need to overcome *any* problem that comes up in your life through Christ, including your struggle with weight.

Don't let those lies sneak in and convince you of anything else. The truth is, you don't have to be afraid of failing, because with Christ, you are an overcomer and more than a conqueror!

> **Lord**, thank You for giving me the power to overcome any difficulty in my life! I get discouraged so easily when I try so hard and can't seem to make progress. I don't want to fail again. Help me to rest in the truth that You are always faithful. My hope is in You. You have made me more than a conqueror. Amen.

Day 23

SLEEP

❧

"In peace I will lie down and sleep, for you alone, LORD, make me dwell in safety."
- Psalm 4:8

Life is a lot of work. There are bills to pay, bosses to appease, families to feed, conflicts to resolve, and a multitude of other things pulling you in every direction imaginable. Our minds twirl, our hearts ache, and it's no shock when weariness sets in. We fly through our days, trying to squeeze every last bit of energy out of ourselves before we crash for the night.

Sleep tends to be more of a last resort than a significant and worthwhile piece of our lives.

Hard work is wonderful and rewarding, but it needs to be counterbalanced with enough rest to rejuvenate and refuel us. When I wake up exhausted, knowing I didn't get enough rest the night before, my first thought is to reach for a cup of coffee. It's so easy to turn to other things to push ourselves harder and faster in an attempt to keep up with the frantic pace of life. Running through a Starbucks drive thru or grabbing an energy drink seem like the perfect quick fix to that nagging fatigue.

Those things can keep you going for a while, but you can only fight against your nature for so long. God created you with the need for rest, and it just so happens life goes so much more smoothly after a full night of sleep. You are in a better mood. You can think more clearly. You have energy to get through the tasks of your day.

It takes intention and purpose. At the beginning, it seems like such an inconvenience. But it is oh-so worthwhile to give your body the rest it needs and your soul the rest it craves to sleep sweetly in perfect peace.

Lord, thank You for the blessing of sweet and restful sleep. Please, help me to make rest a priority in my life. It is so tempting to keep filling my schedule with just one more thing or pull up Facebook just one more time before bed. In those times, remind me that what I need is more important than what I feel like doing at the time. When I do lie down, God, calm my racing mind and anxious thoughts. Cover me with Your peace. Amen.

Day 24

MORE GRACE

∽❧∾

"But he said to me, "My grace is sufficient for you, for my power is made perfect in weakness." Therefore I will boast all the more gladly about my weaknesses, so that Christ's power may rest on me."
- 2 Corinthians 12:9

I am my own worst critic, and I would venture to guess the same thing is true for you. I hold myself to a standard of perfection when I would never expect the same of anyone else. I am supposed to have the perfect walk with God, a flawless exercise routine, color-coded meal plans, an organized closet, and conflict-free relationships.

When I forget someone's birthday, I feel terribly guilty. When I can't get through my to-do list, I lay on more pressure to work harder the next day. When I unintentionally hurt someone, I beat myself up terribly. The words I speak to myself most often are things like, "Work harder, do better, dig deeper, go faster, push yourself, you're capable of more, you're not doing enough."

It is a wonderful thing to work hard, but you also need to remove the weight of the world from your shoulders and look carefully at your expectations. Your job is not to be everything to everyone. You are not perfect, and that's a good thing, because if you were, why would you need

God? That space between your best and perfection is where God's power shines. He not only fills in our gaps, but His power works *best* in those areas of weakness.

Pull down that mask you've been wearing, trying to prove to everyone you've got it all together. Believe me, you don't. Nobody does! You are going to make mistakes and fall short. Let yourself be real, admit those areas of weakness, and invite Him into those shameful and embarrassing places.

Learn to accept His grace. God's love is not performance-based. Nothing you can do or say can make Him love you any more than He already does. Yes, work hard. Do the best you can, but then let that be good enough and let His grace fill in the gaps.

Lord, thank You for not expecting perfection from me. I am so tired of failing to meet that unreachable goal I set for myself. Teach me to accept Your grace in my life and be willing to admit my mistakes and weaknesses to let Your strength shine through them. Without You, I have nothing, but with You, God, I have everything I could ever need. Amen.

Day 25

PLAN

∽◉◠

"The plans of the diligent lead to profit as surely as haste leads to poverty."   *- Proverbs 21:5*

The grocery store is a dangerousplace for me to be when I don't have a list. Trays of donuts, aisles of cookies, and bags of chips beckon me. Unless I have a meal plan for the week, I will end up walking out of the store with a cart load full of junk food, which I always end up regretting later. Cheetos and chocolate chip cookies don't make for a very satisfying dinner.

Planning our meals allows us to eat the foods we enjoy most, save calories, and save money on groceries. Granted, just because we make a plan doesn't mean everything will fall into place just as expected. Life is unpredictable, and we have to roll with that as well. The important part is staying diligent in our follow-through. Our intentional decisions lead us closer and closer to success. Keep healthy snacks in the house and plan meals with lots of fresh vegetables, fruit, whole grains, and lean proteins.

Whether it is in your weekly schedule, your meal plan, your exercise routine, or your business plan, the right steps don't usually just fall into your lap. It takes time, intentionality, and diligence to work your way toward success. Set yourself up to make those better decisions to move you forward. Use an app on your phone, a planner with colorful pens (my personal favorite), a website printable, a white board, or a Post-It note. It doesn't matter how you do it, just the act of thinking ahead and recording your plan makes such a big difference.

Take the time to plan and, not only will your schedule run more smoothly with less stress, but you will also feel great about making healthy decisions you can be proud of along the way.

Lord, thank You for the ability to think ahead and make plans. My time, my money, and my energy is all Yours, so please give me wisdom in how to use it best to honor You. Show me the plans to make to move towards my goals and live out my purpose.
Help me to prioritize and make time for the important things, and help me turn these plans into action. Amen.

Day 26

LEARN TO LISTEN

Stop drinking only water, and use a little wine because of your stomach and your frequent illnesses.
- 1 Timothy 5:23

Our bodies are so complex, and they give us all sorts of signals all day, every day. If we have a food allergy, we may get hives or stomach pain. If we aren't drinking enough water, we may feel sluggish and get headaches. Our shoulders might tense up when we are stressed. I am especially amazed by pica, a disorder that can be triggered by a lack of iron or zinc, causing us to crave things like dirt or chalk (which happen to contain iron and zinc). Our bodies communicate with us, but we just don't always pay attention!

Do not get so hung up on the rules that you forget to listen to your body. I'm not talking about giving into food cravings because those are usually your emotions trying to guide your actions, not your body telling you what it needs. There are also certainly times, like when your body is sore after a workout, that you shouldn't just stop exercising because it's uncomfortable. I'm talking about slowing down and paying attention more often to the signals your body is sending you.

Are you eating the chips just because they are on the table, or are you actually hungry? Are you finishing those last few bites just to clean your plate, or are you really not full yet? When you get a headache, think about what you've been eating and how much water you've been drinking. A friend of mine all but got rid of her horrible headaches when she started paying attention and realized gluten was a trigger for her. If you have eaten all of your allotted calories for the day and you are still legitimately hungry, then eat a little bit more (of something healthy and satiating, not a cookie!). If you usually sleep 7 hours a night and still wake up exhausted, go to bed earlier for a longer night of rest.

I am a rule follower to my core, but dieting and weight loss "rules" are just general guidelines to help you work toward a healthy lifestyle. Every person's body is different, and you are the only one who knows what yours is telling you, so pay attention!

Lord, thank You for creating such a complex body that can tell me so many things. Help me to slow down, listen, and pay attention. I want to know my body's specific needs so I can take better care of myself. Amen.

Day 27

WATER

～❧～

"Jesus answered, 'Everyone who drinks this water will be thirsty again, but whoever drinks the water I give them will never thirst. Indeed, the water I give them will become in them a spring of water welling up to eternal life.'"   *- John 4:13-14*

Water is our lifeblood, one of the most important basic elements necessary for life. The list of benefits we experience from drinking water is just as long as the list of the dangers of dehydration, but nearly half of Americans still don't drink enough. Why? Why would we not drink one of the most readily available, healthy, and free resources around?

It's so easy to gloss over those advantages when other options are more tempting. We can get a caffeine buzz from a soda or taste the sweet rush of fruit juice. The more we drink them, the more we want to drink them, craving more caffeine and more sweetness. But those drinks, while they taste good in the moment, are not only unhealthy, but they don't actually quench our thirst very well. Plain old water may not taste as good at first when it doesn't give us the sugar rush or caffeine high we desire, but it is the one that will satisfy our body most.

Drinking water is life-sustaining. Water gives us energy, helps curb hunger cravings, prevents sickness, wards away headaches, and so much more. I don't think it's any accident that the Bible references water over 700 times, both literally and figuratively. Jesus offers us "living water" – salvation and eternal life - if we choose to follow Him. He gives us life, heals us, and washes away our sins—all gifts that He freely offers to us!

Just as your body craves water, your soul longs for God. So often, you reject that gift and run to things that seem more appealing, trying harder and harder to fill that emptiness you feel. But in the end, all of these things fall short of what your heart truly longs for because nothing else is able to quench that thirst for true life only God can give. Nothing else satisfies.

Lord, thank You for the thirst-quenching, satisfying gift of water. If I have a dependence on any other drink, help me to break it. I don't want to ignore this essential need I have. I want to fully accept and appreciate this indispensable part of life. You are living water and my soul longs for You above all. Amen.

Day 28

JUST KEEP GOING

❦

*"Let us not become weary in doing good, for at the proper time we
will reap a harvest if we do not give up."*
- Galatians 6:9

Time is the worst enemy of enthusiasm. When we start something new and it's still shiny and exciting, it doesn't take much work to get going, but to keep it going? Well, that's an entirely different story.

When we don't get immediate results, we grow weary pretty quickly. What do you mean I caught a cold? I ate a salad yesterday and vegetables are supposed to boost my immune system! I exercised for half an hour every day this week, and I still haven't reached my goal weight? Outrageous! It's not worth the effort! We live in a culture of instant gratification teaching us to expect to get what we want right when we want it. There's something extremely important missing from that equation – patience.

It's easy to give up when things don't go your way, but just because you aren't seeing the results, doesn't mean they aren't there. God knows how much you struggle in that area and tells you exactly what to do - Don't give up. You may not have seen the results yet, but they are coming! Stay on course and persevere.

Often, the things that take the most time and effort bring the most rewarding results. If you stopped watering an apple seed after a week when you didn't see a sprout, you would miss out on the towering tree and all of the fruit that is still to come! Don't give up. It will be hard. It will take patience and endurance and you will be tempted to stop trying. Don't give up. The best is yet to come.

Lord, thank You for constantly working in my life, when I can see it and when I can't. Help me to grow my patience when I'm working hard and just feel like giving up. Replace my discouragement with hope, and my frustration with great expectations for the things yet to come. Give me the strength to persevere, one day at a time. Amen.

Day 29

IT'S NOT ABOUT THE WEIGHT

But I have raised you up for this very purpose, that I might show you
my power and that my name might be proclaimed in all the earth.
- Exodus 9:16

I t's not about the weight. I know that sounds odd coming from
someone who claims losing 100 pounds has changed her life, but it's
true. I spent years thinking the only reason I couldn't attract guys,
didn't feel good in my clothes, and couldn't keep up on bike rides with
friends was because I was overweight.

It turns out, the weight wasn't really to blame. Those extra pounds were
part of it, but it was really just a symptom of something else going on that
was preventing me from living a life of true freedom in Christ. For me,
that chain was rooted in my insecurities. I didn't feel good enough, strong
enough, thin enough, or just *enough* in general. I believed all kinds of lies
about my identity, though I didn't know they were lies at the time.

When our identity isn't firmly rooted in Christ, it's like grasping at straws
to try to fill in the gaps. Our beliefs about what we look like, what we are
capable of, and how everyone else sees us can either keep us trapped in a
tiny little box or set us free to live our lives to the fullest.

Stop looking to the scale to define your worth, or even your mood. Choose to stand taller, try new things, and leave that comfortable spot watching from the sidelines to join the activities of life. Don't miss out on experiencing life with the people you love.

It's not about the weight. It's about living a life of purpose. It's about knowing, without a doubt, how deep and wide your Heavenly Father loves you. You were lovingly created for a powerful reason. You were made to make an impact on this world in a way nobody else can, so break through those chains of whatever is holding you back from your divine purpose and go live out your calling!

Lord, thank You for raising me up for a purpose – to proclaim Your name to all the earth.

I have kept my voice quiet for far too long because I just felt inadequate for such an important job. Overcome my fears and cast out my insecurities so I can find my identity only in You. Build me up, teach me, and empower me to use my body and my life to bring glory and honor to You in all that I do. Let them see You in me. Amen.

Day 30

FINDING FREEDOM

≈≈≈

It is for freedom that Christ has set us free. Stand firm, then, and do not let yourselves be burdened again by a yoke of slavery.
- Galatians 5:1

Do you remember learning to read? It is a tough thing to master the English language. Once we get past learning the sight words, we have to memorize rules like "i before e" and the difference between long and short vowel sounds. When we add on all of the exceptions to the rules, it is sure a lot to remember! It takes tremendous effort just to stumble our way through a short sentence, trying to remember all of that information at the same time! It's difficult and frustrating, but then something starts to happen. We read that sentence again and again, and it gets easier.

We don't have to think about all of those rules anymore because our brains recognize those letters on the page and know how to make sense of them now! We needed the rules to get us started, to teach ourselves what to do with all of that information. Now that we have that part figured out, we can move on to easy readers, then chapter books, then novels and plays. We become free to read whatever our hearts desire!

You can find that same kind of freedom in a healthy lifestyle! There is a lifestyle out there that allows you to eat foods you love when you feel hungry and gives you the power to stop eating when you are full, leaving you nourished and satisfied. It is possible to be healthy without counting every calorie and gram of fat you eat. You can feel comfortable in your own skin and move and play, not because you have to for weight loss, but because you enjoy it and you want to! You do have to invest the time and effort into learning how to make healthy food and exercise choices. You need to learn the rules that teach you how to put together a balanced diet and pay attention to the recommendations that tell you how much you should be moving.

It is difficult and frustrating at first, but then something starts to happen. You start making those choices again and again, and it gets easier. You don't have to think about it as much because it's just the way you live now! It's not about the rules anymore, it's about what those rules taught you to be able to do – to make the decisions, one by one, which will lead you to freedom!

> **Lord**, I have been bound by the chains of food cravings, insecurities, and weight struggles for far too long. I don't want to be held back by those things anymore! Help me to find that freedom in You, one decision at a time, as You break through every chain in my life and make me an overcomer. Amen.